This book of miracles belongs to:

STRENGTHEN YOUR FAITH THROUGH JOURNALING.

Faith journaling, or Bible journaling, is a way of exploring your faith creatively.
You can write or draw, use art supplies or office supplies, write in a Bible or
a notebook…whatever feels right for your journey. The prompts in this book
can help you get started. By taking the time to sit down and engage with them,
you'll feel more connected to God. So set aside some time for yourself and your
journal, and turn the page. May it be a valuable step on your faith journey.

"The moment I connected my faith
to my creativity, everything changed."

–Shanna Noel–

creator of Illustrated Faith
(*www.illustratedfaith.com*)

Carve out a few minutes to consider and be grateful
for your home and family. How is your home blessed?
What do you love about it?

Friends love all the time,
and kinsfolk are born
for times of trouble.

Proverbs 17:17

I have no greater joy
than this: to hear that
my children are living
according to the truth.

3 John 1:4

How your day begins can have a huge effect on how it goes.
What is your family's morning routine?
How does it support your bodies, minds, and souls?
If you could change one thing about it, what would it be?

_____

_____

_____

_____

_____

_____

_____

_____

_____

_____

_____

_____

_____

_____

_____

_____

AS FOR ME AND MY HOUSE, WE WILL SERVE the LORD.

JOSHUA 24:15

This is the day
the LORD acted;
we will rejoice and
celebrate in it!

Psalm 118:24

find Strength in
faith &
family

There are many, many ways—large and small—to find strength
in faith and family. How do you find strength in yours?
Think about it in reverse, too: how do you strengthen your family?

Rushing waters
can't quench love;
rivers can't
wash it away.

Song of Solomon 8:7

23

Every good gift, every perfect
gift, comes from above.
These gifts come down from
the Father, the creator
of the heavenly lights,
in whose character there
is no change at all.

James 1:17

Think about the people in your life for whom you are grateful. They could be people you see every day or once in awhile; they could even be long gone from your life. Who are they?

Now faith, hope,
and love remain—
these three things—
and the greatest
of these is love.

1 Corinthians 13:13

Though love may be the greatest of the three, faith and hope
are vital to your relationships with your loved ones.
What do they mean to you in regard to your family?

Faith is the reality
of what we hope for,
the proof of
what we don't see.

Hebrews 11:1

God has the power to provide
you with more than enough
of every kind of grace.
That way, you will have
everything you need …
for every kind of good work.

2 Corinthians 9:8

As you go about your daily routines and chores at home,
take the opportunity to think about your prayers for your home.
What are they? What would you like your home to be?

Instead, like a newborn baby,
desire the pure milk of the
word. Nourished by it,
you will grow into salvation,
since you have tasted that
the Lord is good.

1 Peter 2:2-3

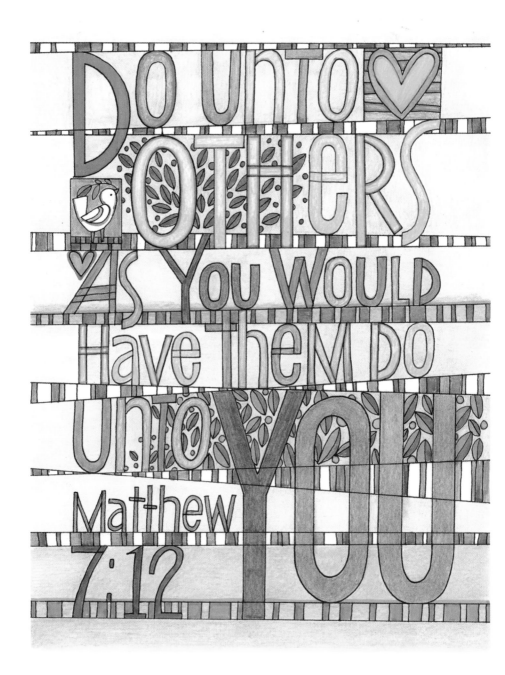

Do unto others as you would have them do unto you

Matthew 7:12

Doing unto others as you would like them to do unto you can be much more difficult than it sounds. Often we don't even realize when we're not. Think of someone you find frustrating.
Do you treat them as you would like to be treated?
How could you do better?

Dear friends, let's love each other, because love is from God, and everyone who loves is born from God and knows God.

1 John 4:7

As a mother
comforts her child,
so I will comfort you;
in Jerusalem you
will be comforted.

Isaiah 66:13

58

Think about the good things you sow in the world and—as honestly as you can—consider the bad things. What new habits could you sow? What should you stop sowing?

whatever one sows,

GALATIANS 6:7

that will he also Reap

61

Train children in the way
they should go;
when they grow old, they
won't depart from it.

Proverbs 22:6

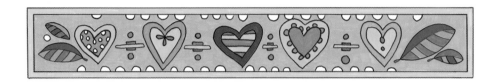

Let all that you do be done in

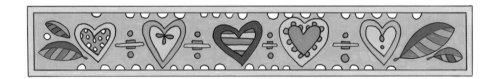

Every family has arguments. The important thing is to let all that you do—even arguing—be done in love. What do moments like this look like in your family? How are they handled?
How can you move forward together?

_____

_____

_____

_____

_____

_____

_____

_____

_____

_____

_____

_____

_____

_____

_____

Be kind, compassionate,
and forgiving to each
other, in the same way God
forgave you in Christ.

Ephesians 4:32

Love puts up with all things,
trusts in all things,
hopes for all things,
endures all things.
Love never fails.

1 Corinthians 13:7-8

Forgiveness expands the heart, and it goes both ways. Who do you need to forgive? Could you do it? If you could ask for forgiveness from any person you know, alive or dead, who would it be?

If you forgive others
their sins, your heavenly
Father will also forgive you.

Matthew 6:14

with God
all things
are possible.

MATTHEW 19:26

How we live can teach others so much, just by example. Who are the people who look up to you? They might be children or young adults, or perhaps they're friends or family members who respect or admire you. What values would you like to show them?

Remember your leaders who spoke God's word to you. Imitate their faith as you consider the way their lives turned out.

Hebrews 13:7

More than anything
you guard, protect
your mind, for life
flows from it.

Proverbs 4:23

Sometimes we hold ourselves back from acting on—or even considering—certain changes to our lives because we know there's a good chance they'll fail. Do you have anything like that? If you knew it would not fail, what is one thing you would do to improve your family's home life?

GOD is Within Her She Will Not fall

Psalm 46:5

But the fruit of the Spirit
is love, joy, peace, patience,
kindness, goodness,
faithfulness, gentleness,
and self-control.

Galatians 5:22-23

Spend some time reflecting on the fruit of the Spirit, and be thankful for the love, joy, peace, patience, kindness, goodness, faithfulness, gentleness, and self-control in your life.
How can you nurture them in your family?

Let's not get tired
of doing good, because
in time we'll have a harvest
if we don't give up.

Galatians 6:9

So continue encouraging
each other and building
each other up, just like
you are doing already.

1 Thessalonians 5:11

What are your biggest prayers for your family as a whole?
What about for each of your family members?
Don't forget to include yourself.

_____

_____

_____

_____

_____

_____

_____

_____

_____

_____

_____

_____

_____

_____

_____

_____

Therefore I say to you,
whatever you pray and ask for,
believe that you will receive it,
and it will be so for you.

Mark 11:24

Burst forth in Beauty & Radiant Love

Spend a few minutes reflecting on and being thankful for the gifts that God has given you. How do you use them to help others? Don't forget the small ways—sometimes the smallest work you do has the largest impact on someone else.

The second is this,
You will love your
neighbor as yourself.
No other commandment is
greater than these.

Mark 12:31

Don't forget to do good and
to share what you have
because God is pleased with
these kinds of sacrifices.

Hebrews 13:16

Your family naturally grows—in size, sometimes, but also as individuals—over the years. How do you picture them in five years? Ten? How can you grow together?

Carry each other's
burdens and so you
will fulfill the
law of Christ.

Galatians 6:2

ABOUT THE ARTIST

Robin Pickens grew up in a creative family, making drawing and art a natural choice for her. After earning her BFA from the University of Michigan School of Art, Robin worked for many years as a successful broadcast television art director and animator. She then chose to pursue her passion for creating art that speaks from her heart and reflects her creative life as a wife and mother. Robin licenses her artwork for a variety of products, including Christmas ornaments, fabrics, calendars, greeting cards, gift books, home décor, wall art, dishware, and more. You can find more of Robin's work at *www.spoonflower.com/profiles/robinpickens* as well as through her website, *www.robinpickens.com.*

ISBN 978-1-64178-000-1

Fox Chapel Publishing makes every effort to use environmentally friendly paper for printing.

© 2018 by Robin Pickens and Quiet Fox Designs; *www.QuietFoxDesigns.com*, an imprint of Fox Chapel Publishing, 800-457-9112, 903 Square Street, Mount Joy, PA 17552.

We are always looking for talented authors. To submit an idea, please send a brief inquiry to acquisitions@foxchapelpublishing.com.

Printed in China
First printing